Naples
FLORIDA

A PHOTOGRAPHIC PORTRAIT

PHOTOGRAPHY BY RANDALL PERRY
NARRATIVE BY JEAN AMODEA

TWIN LIGHTS PUBLISHERS, ROCKPORT, MASSACHUSETTS

First published in the United States of
America by:

Twin Lights Publishers, Inc.
51 Broadway
Rockport, Massachusetts 01966
Telephone: (978) 546-7398
www.twinlightspub.com

ISBN: 978-1-934907-32-0

10 9 8 7 6 5 4 3

Images and captions on pages 30–31
provided by the Naples Historical Society.

(opposite)
Lowdermilk Park Beach

(frontispiece)
Snowy Egret

(jacket front)
Doctors Pass Waterway

(jacket back)
Park Shore Beach
Fifth Avenue

Book design by:
SYP Design & Production, Inc.
www.sypdesign.com

Printed in China

NAPLES ON THE GULF

Known as Florida's "crown jewel," Naples is located on the sun-drenched, southwest Gulf Coast of Florida, in Collier County. With its shimmering sugar-white sand beaches, placid surf and glistening blue skies, discriminating travelers consider it the premier resort destination. Echoed repeatedly by locals, vacationers, and "snow birds" with seasonal residences, being in Naples is the closest to experiencing all that is imagined as paradise due to its idyllic climate. Sub-tropical, sunny days are year-round and serve to enable lush vegetation to proliferate and wildlife to thrive.

Year-round, outdoor enthusiasts revel in the abundance of water sports, boating, deep sea fishing, swimming, shell collecting, and dolphin and manatee sightseeing cruises. With world-class, championship golf greens in what some say is the golf capital of the world, Naples boasts the second-most golf holes per capita than anywhere else.

The wonder of spotting Naples' estuary wildlife, marine animals, land and seabirds winging through their natural habitats makes Naples a beloved destination for flora and fauna devotees.

Sighting one of 350 pairs of bald eagles, or an American alligator, languid sea turtles, Florida panthers to graceful dolphins and wintering manatees make the area a bonanza for eco-tourists.

Extraordinary cultural and art offerings abound with theater venues, art galleries, museums, fine jewelry and antique shops and Naples' own center for the arts, Artis-Naples that houses the Naples Philharmonic Orchestra and The Baker Museum of Art.

For shoppers, a dizzying array of exquisite options await, from Olde Naples' Third Street South to fashionable downtown 5th Avenue, mid-town to The Village on Venetian Bay and the chic boutiques at the Waterside Shops and north to the newest, shopping destination, Mercato.

Enjoy this extraordinary photographic journey and be mesmerized by Randall Perry's visual chronicle of this city as he captures its spirit and culture in *Naples: A Photographic Portrait*.

Trinity-by-the-Cove (opposite)

Trinity-by-the-Cove dates back to 1949 when a group of parishioners gathered at the original Naples Beach Hotel. The composed symmetry of the church's exterior reflects the glory of its inner spiritual life via vibrant services. Seasonal presentations include the 14-voice vocal ensemble and classical music concerts.

Naples Pier

Erected in 1888, this iconic attraction is known both as Naples Fishing Pier and Naples Municipal Pier. In the early twentieth century, narrow gauge train rails were used on its deck to transport baggage and freight from boats bringing early "snow birds." Today, visitors enjoy strolling its 1,000-foot length.

Key West Style Cottage (top)

Charming and oh so cozy cottages located in downtown Naples are available for purchase or rental by the week or season. Situated within an easy bike ride or walk to the nearby beach, these quiet retreats on streets lined with lush foliage are the perfect get-aways for vacationers.

Knight Anole (bottom)

Southwest Floridians share their sub-tropical paradise with some 10 native species of lizards like the Knight Anole. Found in trees and sunning on branches, they are lime green with large heads and a yellow stripe on the side of their neck. They grow up to 20 inches and can live up to 16 years.

Easy, Breezy Living (opposite)

Reminiscent of a Thomas McKnight painting bedecked in white, pale hues and shades of deep blue, laid-back Naples living is effortless and the norm. Relax with a chilled afternoon cocktail in preparation of welcoming another dazzling sunset from the balcony of a private Key West style cottage.

Boathouses of Yesteryear *(above)*

Located in Port Royal, these boathouses originally housed vessels of prominent citizens, without after-boating amenities. Today, modern boathouses like Naples Boat Club, provide state-of-the-art wet slip marinas and dry rack boat storage with nearby dining options, yacht brokerage, and sales services.

Doctors Pass Waterway
(opposite, top and bottom)

Locally known as the "middle pass," it is one of three principle passes along with Gordon Pass and Wiggins Pass that provides clearance and boating access to the Gulf of Mexico. The pass is bordered by Park Shore, The Moorings, and Coquina Sands.

Kayaking *(above and opposite, bottom)*

Nature lovers take advantage of excursions via kayaks available as singles, tandems, sit-on-tops or fish and dive types that allow you to sit inches from the water for premium close-up views. Fishing the brackish waters of the Cocohatchee River from a kayak provides excellent snook and redfish catches.

Pelicans and More (top)

Pelicans and other wildlife are a treasured part of Naples' environment. For wildlife in need, the staff at the Conservancy Wildlife Clinic at the Sharon and Dolph von Arx Wildlife Hospital at the Conservancy of Southwest Florida care for thousands of species yearly with half released back into native habitats.

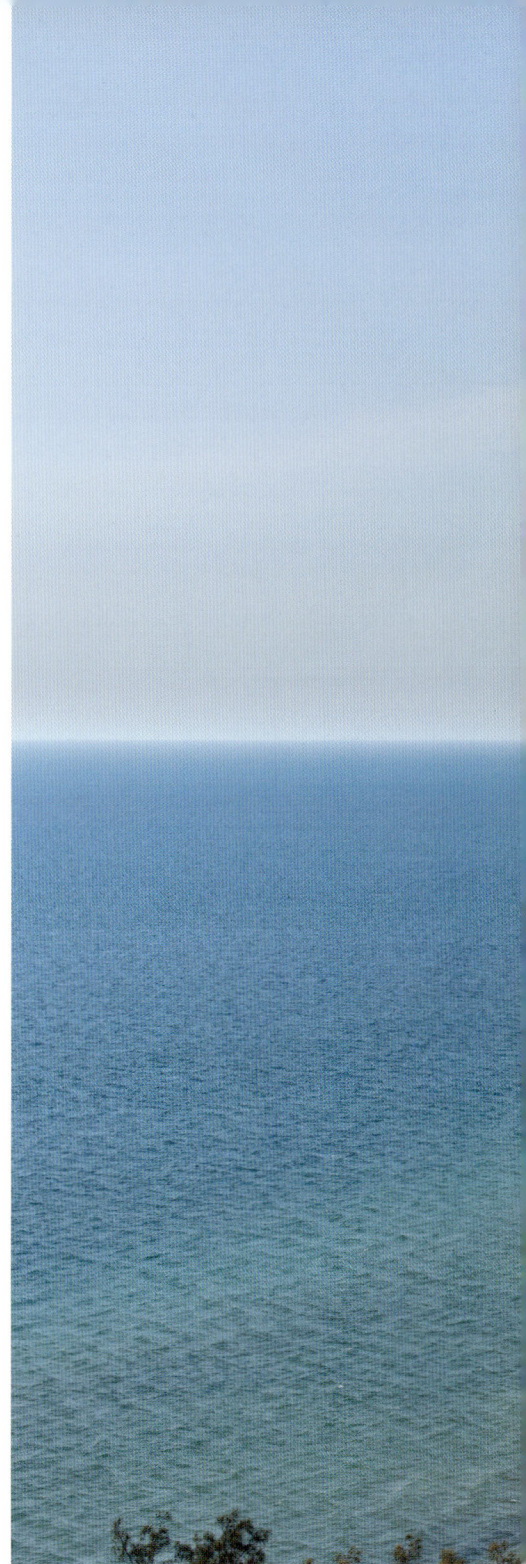

Pier Beach Access

Metered parking and spots for the handicapped are on nearly every block in Olde Naples, providing easy passage via sandy paths to gorgeous beaches located on each side of Naples Pier. Whether enjoying lunch, sunning or just strolling along the water's edge, the pier beaches are a must-visit spot.

Park Shore Beach Area

Located north of the Moorings and in close proximity to the heart of Naples' main attractions, Park Shore is a combination of condos, single family dwellings, and bay and beach homes in a development that was constructed in the late 60's and early 70's.

Lowdermilk Beach Park (top)

Lowdermilk Beach Park is especially popular in the winter season. Couples desirous of an idyllic wedding destination pledge their troth under clear blue skies and balmy temperatures. Afterwards, many die-hard sun and sand lovers celebrate their special day with catered luncheons right on the beach.

Kite Surfing (bottom)

Surface water sports like kite surfing are among the most popular Naples' water pastimes. Powered by the wind, air currents waft and lift power kites that dot the air with color and the promise of a heart-pounding ride.

Peaceful Early Mornings (opposite)

Quiet walks on the park's sugar white sand or green grass knolls are best in early morning before beach lovers claim their spot for the day. While the sun shines most every day from late fall through spring, mean temperatures during winter hover around 72 degrees and dip to 53 degrees in the evenings.

A Walker's Delight

Fitness aficionados and casual strollers enjoy daily leisurely walks on Naples' pristine beaches. Shelling, a popular pastime, fetches specimens, some intact, such as conches, whelks, and scallops. Especially coveted are the sun-bleached sand dollars that once inhabited the Gulf's soft, sandy bottom.

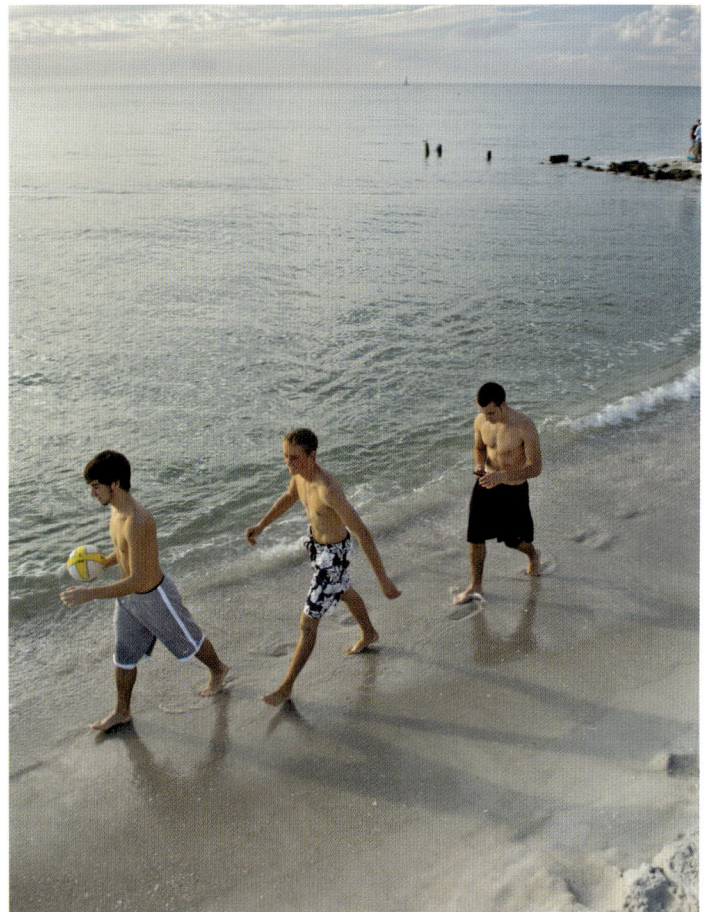

For Play and Picnics *(above and right)*

Considered one of the "most popular public beaches in Naples," teens can work up an appetite after an afternoon of play at one of the park's volleyball courts. Kiddies can tire out at the playground, then lunch at beachside pavilions or under tiki huts and finish the day with a quiet beach stroll.

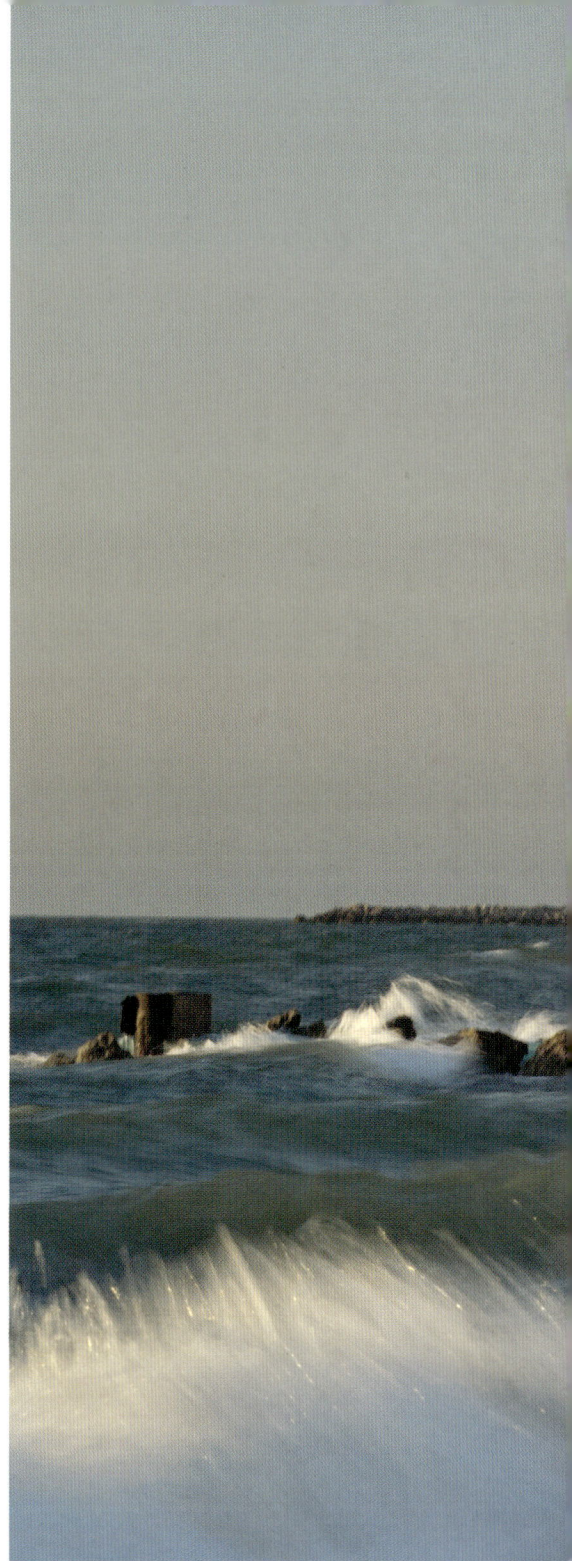

Lowdermilk Beach Park (top)

With all the amenities needed for a day of sun and surf, Lowdermilk Beach Park attracts visitors 365 days a year. A family-friendly beach with a duck pond and jungle-gym playground, a snack bar, picnic tables, gazebo, restrooms and showers, Lowdermilk Beach Park is an iconic Naples area destination.

A Venue for Exercise Lovers (bottom)

Early mornings find fitness enthusiasts claiming the park for their own. From triathlon trainers who discipline themselves for the arduous challenge of swimming and traversing through beach sand to those who relish a brisk early morning swim, the park attracts outdoor enthusiasts of all persuasions.

Naples' Beaches

Nothing short of extraordinary, Naples' semi-tropical weather and white beaches are coveted by sand and surf lovers both in the states and abroad. With some 450,000 residents, the population swells to more than 600,000 in the peak of the season. Miles of beach access makes it a water lover's paradise.

Water Recreational Park

Located within North Collier Regional Park, Sun-N-Fun Lagoon is a popular waterpark that features water fountains that shoot up from the pavement, five totally enclosed water slides with a seven-second drop to the pool below, as well as a winding river ride, a kiddy pool, an activity pool, and a diving area.

From the Air

Water temperatures of rides and attractions constantly adjust to a comfortable 84 degrees. Lifeguards are on duty and a first aid station is at the ready if needed. After working up an appetite, visit the Snack Shack for a bite and cold drink, and finish with a refreshing shower in the guest locker rooms.

Doctors Pass Waterway

Local anglers consider this a hot spot
for reeling in prized specimens like
tarpon and Spanish mackerel fished
off the beaches along the coastline.
According to local lore, the pass is said
to have been named after an unknown
doctor who was the sole survivor of a
sailing accident.

Naples Beach at Twilight

Beachgoers enjoy a stroll along Naples Beach at twilight. The soft diffused light, warm water and tranquil Gulf breeze attracts both residents and visitors year-round. With over ten miles of white sandy beach and clear shallow water, it is a perfect spot for a refreshing evening dip.

Naples Pier Sunset

Heralding the close of another day, a must-see event for visitors and coveted by fortunate locals year-round, is the iconic Naples sunset. As the sun makes its slow descent and dips headfirst into the Gulf, fishermen anxiously cast lines for the last of the day's catch, and visitors claim their spot on the pier to witness nature's adieu to another perfect day.

Ready for the Links *(top)*

Golfers arise to a misty morning tee time and the promise of another day of spectacular play. A paradise for golfers, Naples boasts more courses per capita that can be found globally. Golf communities abound, designed by luminaries such as Greg Norman, Jack Nicklaus, Tom Fazio, and Arnold Palmer.

Country Club Style Living *(bottom)*

Likened to a first-class resort, member-owned Wyndemere Country Club has 634 residences that include condominiums, villas, single family, and estate homes. An active social calendar features events that start with a "Welcome Back" event and continues throughout the season's holiday calendar.

Idyllic Golfing *(top)*

With average temperatures ranging from the mid 70's to low 80's during Southwest Florida winters and with an average monthly rain fall of two inches, golfing enthusiasts nationwide flock to the area. With greens that are slick and true and meticulously manicured, the area leads as a golf destination.

Golfing Bliss *(bottom)*

Naples has over 80 courses known for the best in play for all levels from value-priced courses like Valencia Golf and Country Club to more pricey courses like Tiburon Golf Club. The latter, a Greg Norman designed 27-hole course, is the site of well-attended Franklin Templeton Shootout, celebrating its 25th year.

29

Historic Palm Cottage

The Cottage, Naples' oldest house (1895) is the educational headquarters for Naples Historical Society. Fifteen thousand plus visitors encounter Naples history annually through 12 programs and initiatives. The Cottage, a Landmark in the National Register of Historic Places, is a 3,500 square foot museum showcasing tours throughout the year.

The Norris Gardens

The Gardens at Historic Palm Cottage are not historic but the collection offers visitors a glimpse into the past through history lessons told through a "garden lens." An Oval Lawn complemented by five gardens and a chickee, The Gardens give visitors a welcome opportunity to relax and reflect on Naples' past.

Quaint Cottages

Olde Naples historic district is a coveted vacation spot for those looking for charming and tranquil hideaways. Luxury cottages that exude a beach ambiance, outfitted with natural materials like bamboo, sea grass, and rattan with updated amenities are available for rent year-round.

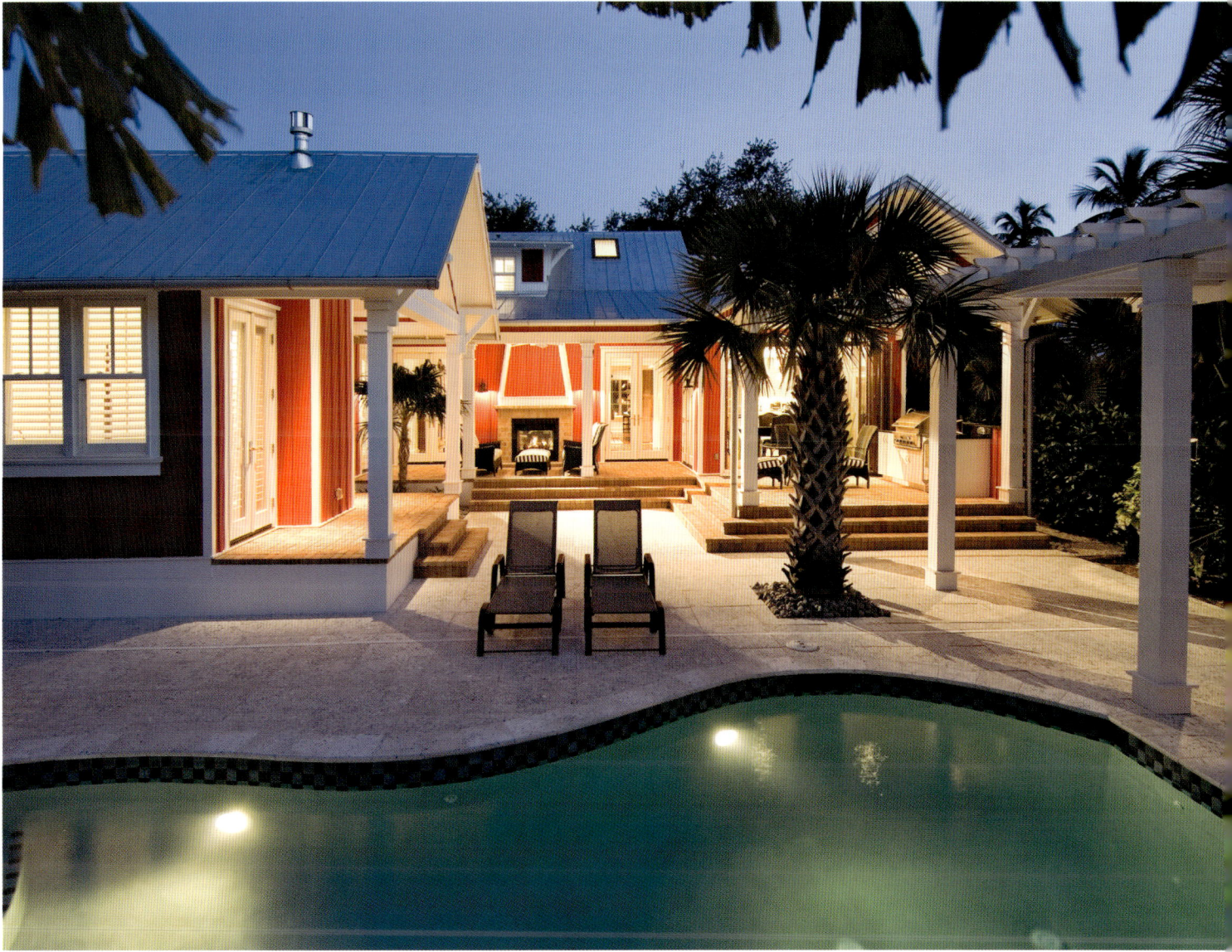

Residences with Appeal *(above)*

Whether you relax poolside within the seclusion of your lanai or decide to pack a lunch and walk a few blocks to enjoy a day at the Gulf beaches, downtown Naples' cottages score high in relaxation appeal. Many dwellings provide areas for casual al fresco living and entertaining with outdoor kitchens and fire pits for cozy conversation.

Red-hued Blooms *(right)*

More commonly known as an Egyptian star cluster or star flower, pentas thrive in hot and humid, sandy Florida soil. An evergreen, it grows 24 to 36 inches tall and craves sun to partial shade. Velvet, fuzzy textured foliage supports blooms in shades of near white to lavender, blue-violet, red, and pink.

Water, Water Everywhere *(opposite)*

Relaxing water views, whether from a private home balcony or a high-rise overlooking the Naples Bay or Gulf, provide hours of pleasurable experiences such as bird watching. Spot the state bird, the mockingbird or flocks of heron or coastal birds like hungry gulls, brown pelicans, and frigates.

Swimming Year-round *(top and bottom)*

Backyards and lanais throughout Naples sport architecturally pleasing swimming pools of all sizes and shapes, many with built-in spas. While locals don sweaters, visitors from northern states and abroad are delighted to escape the winter chill by taking a dip in the heated waters.

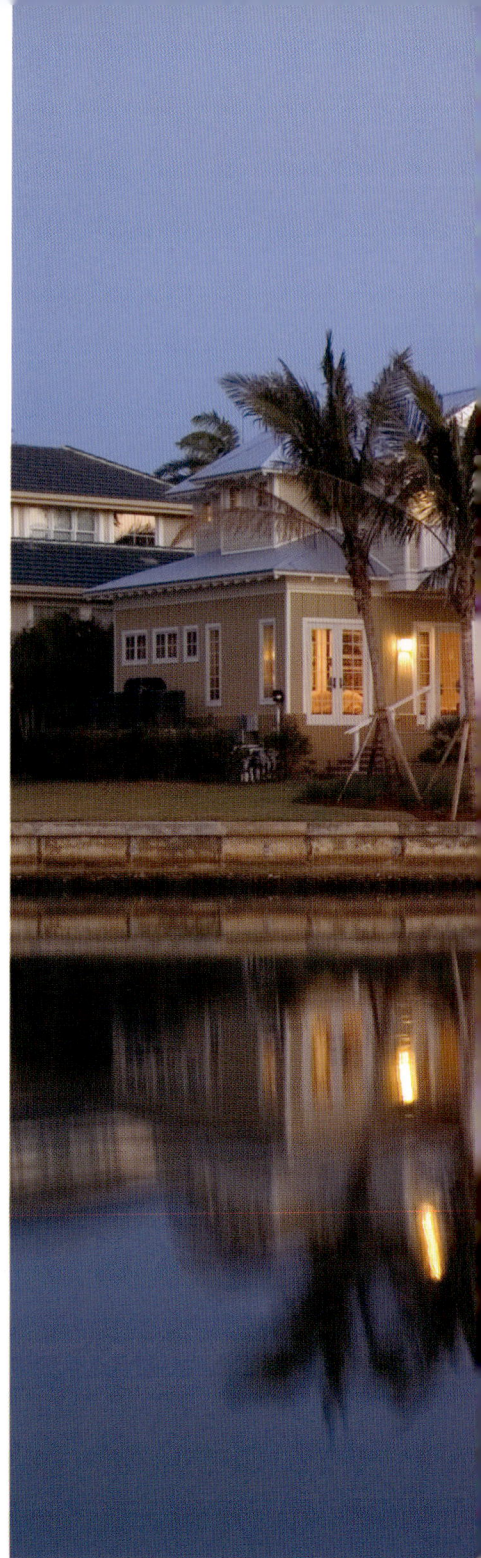

Estates and Mansions

Magnificent homes in the prestigious
Port Royal section boast a private country
club, complete with nine tennis courts,
formal and informal dining facilities,
an Olympic pool, and a vibrant social
calendar. Street names like Rum Row
and Spyglass Lane are evocative of
pirates who once frequented the area.

Waterside Luxe Living

An especially picturesque view of private waterside estate homes that line the Gulf side of the Port Royal section is possible from on-board the *Naples Princess*, a 105-foot-long luxury yacht. Daily sightseeing, sunset, and dinner cruises depart from Port O' Call Marina.

Convenient Gulf Access

Private boat docks lie deserted during Naples' summers, but after mid-October, the pace picks up as "snow birds" return to relax, unwind, refresh, and enjoy Florida living at its finest. Waterfront property owners can launch their crafts from their own docks and quickly access the sparkling Gulf waters.

Bayfront *(top and bottom)*

Erected with European style architecture, Bayfront is a Naples landmark situated at the end of Goodlette-Frank Road and US 41, in downtown Naples. Residences share space with waterside gourmet restaurants and quaint shops outfitted in imported stone on brick-lined walkways.

Naples Bay Resort

Rated four diamonds, the luxurious Naples Bay Resort, designed with colorful, Tuscan-inspired style, rests on Naples Bay. It features a 97-slip marina, from which owners can stay aboard, a Euro-style spa, upscale waterfront shopping, dining, four pools, and a state-of-the-art fitness and tennis facility.

Retirement, Naples Style

For premier assisted living, Moorings Park Retirement Community is the only A+ Fitch rated continuing care retirement community, nationwide. A host of stimulating indoor social activities allows residents to interact, keeping minds and body active.

Distinctive Service and Quality *(above)*

Offering casual and fine dining at the Moorings, residents receive a balanced menu, daily. Activity levels are kept high with brisk swims in the heated pool or play at the 18-hole putting and chipping green. After meals, residents take leisurely strolls on walking paths or to the lakeside.

Native Plant *(right)*

The bromeliad is more commonly called the cardinal air plant, a name inspired by the plant's red floral bracts. The species is abundant on large trees, requiring their moist shelter. Not parasitic on their host trees, for nourishment, bromeliads simply root on the branches and take in nutrients from the air and debris found on the trunks.

Bay Colony Entrance (top)

Located on the Cocohatchee Strand Nature Preserve, Bay Colony is one of the area's most prestigious luxury residences. The clubhouse, built with the grace of a southern plantation, offers dining choices including alfresco. Golf in a manicured, natural setting is exceptional and without tee times.

Gulf Shore Boulevard (bottom)

Parallel to the Gulf shore, this impressive boulevard begins in Olde Naples and runs north to the Vanderbilt Beach area. It features some of the finest waterfront condos, bay homes, and villas in Naples. Residents enjoy tree-lined streets and meridians as well as public entryways that access Gulf beaches.

Riding for Freedom

A Naples landmark since 1992, Frederick Remington's *Lely Freedom Horses* monument graces the entrance of the 3,000-acre Lely Resort in southeast Naples. Included are three championship golf courses, as well as The Players Club & Spa, a 26,000-square-foot fitness and recreational facility.

Tennis Anyone? *(above)*

The premier choice for upscale living, Pelican Bay lies between three miles of sparkling Gulf front beaches to the west and Tamiami Trail to the east on 2,104 acres of natural habitat. Tennis, a favorite sport of Neapolitans, is available to residents at Commons Park with ten tennis courts and at Hammock Oak Park with eight courts.

Pelican Bay *(left and opposite)*

Located north of Naples and directly on the Gulf of Mexico, Pelican Bay consists of roughly 3.29 square miles. Upscale high-rise condominiums, single family homes, coach homes and villa residents enjoy golf, private beach access and beach pavilions, nearby shopping at the Waterside Shops and share real-estate with Artis-Naples center for the performing arts.

Cambier Park Tennis (above)

Open to the public, the fully staffed, full-service Allen Tennis Center features 12 state of the art Hydro-Grid lighted Har-Tru courts. Its Junior Program offers instruction to children ages 4-16 and excels in developing players with good attitudes along with great tennis technique.

Cambier Park (opposite, top and bottom)

Keeping youngsters busy is child's play at Cambier Park. Dual playgrounds —one for under age five and one for older youngsters — entertains along with swings, a hand operated sand digger, and climbing atop pirate ship-like structures. The park has a softball field and a baseball diamond.

Trieste *(above)*

Trieste is the final luxury 19-story tower at Bay Colony. All 105 lavish residences are in close proximity to the beach and feature unparalleled Gulf, bay, and preserve views from elegant three bedroom plus den or four bedroom opulent living quarters.

Bougainvillea Blossoms *(left)*

One of the more dramatic and beautiful of tropical vines used in abundance to enhance outdoor vistas in Naples, the bougainvillea is a large-sized plant that climbs from 10 to 40 feet. Large clusters of papery bracts come in vibrant shades of pink, lavender, red, gold, or orange with many varieties bearing sharp, skin-piercing spines.

Trieste Bay Colony

Enter the tower and experience the grand salon outfitted with hand-stenciled ceilings and a 20-foot-high window that overlooks a majestic fountain. Outdoors, private cabanas tucked amid tropical foliage and a gushing waterfall lends a laidback ambiance that is both sophisticated and casual.

Band Shell Performances (above)

Located in Cambier Park, a key city cultural center, the Cambier Park Band Shell is the site of performances from 1940's big-band concerts to bluegrass bands to Shakespeare in the Park. With acoustics sufficient to serve audiences up to 7,000, music lovers pack the venue in season to see local and national musical acts like the Four Freshmen.

Cambier Park Donors (left)

Thanks to donations and matching grants of generous Neapolitans, facilities and cultural offerings at Cambier Park are thriving. Outdoor movie night with a two story inflatable screen delights young and old alike. Art festivals and music concerts draw throngs from October to January.

The Art of Dance

Naples Academy of Ballet is dedicated to educating, inspiring, and transforming dancers of all ages by providing them with the highest level of professional ballet training in the Naples area. The Studio teaches the traditions and discipline of the Russian Vaganova method.

Sightseeing, Trolley-style *(above)*

Forget driving. Opt for a two hour AAA-rated sightseeing trolley tour aboard the Naples Trolley. Your driver will narrate in colorful detail, Naples' rich history and lore by stopping at over 100 points of interest. It's a must-do activity for new visitors to get familiarized with Naples' best-loved spots from Third Street South, north to Vanderbilt Beach Road.

Naples Trolley *(left)*

The Naples Trolley alligator mascot is representative of the scintillating adventure that waits aboard the popular everglades excursion tour in the comfort-controlled Safari Wagon. A knowledgeable eco-trained navigator provides information about the abundant natural wildlife.

Overview of Naples

Board the trolley at any one of 27 points and exit and tour, shop or dine at your own liking. The tour covers 31 miles that includes stops at Tin City, Port-O-Call Marina, The Dock Restaurant, the Waterside Shops, top country clubs and hotels like the Ritz-Carlton Beach Resort.

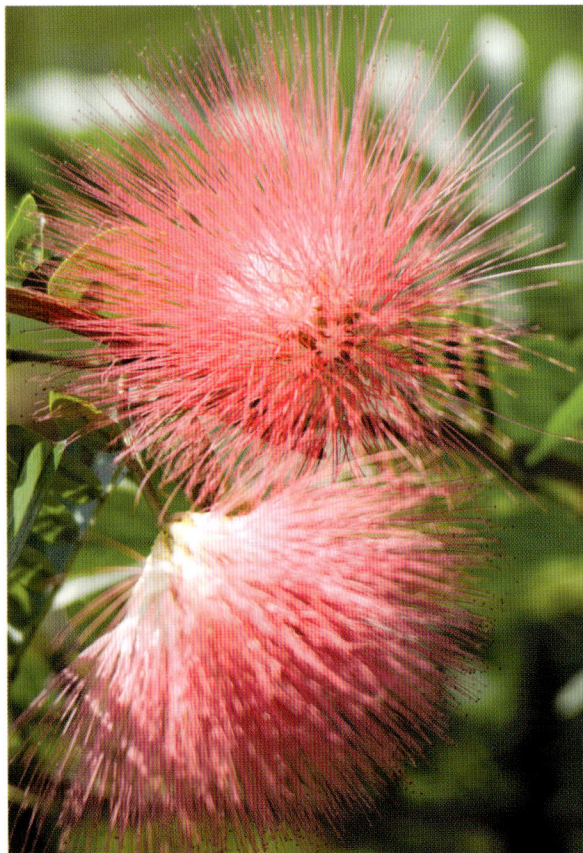

Tuscany-inspired Dining

(above and opposite)

Finding fine dining on Third Street South is a breeze. Campiello's Restaurant, opened in 1998, has been serving innovative, rustic Tuscan-inspired cuisine to the delight of tourists and locals alike. The open kitchen serves up wood-roasted and grilled specialties best enjoyed in an interior inspired by the Michelangelo-designed Villa San Michele, in Fiesole, Italy.

Plants and Fauna *(left)*

The mimosa tree in bloom has a burst of fluffy, pink colored pompom-like, fragrant flowers that are dazzling. The sub-tropical deciduous tree can reach up to 40 feet in height and is grown for its umbrella-shaped canopy. Fernlike, pale-green foliage takes center stage when blooms cease to adorn their host.

Art, Antiques, and More

A fine art destination and a panacea for art enthusiasts, "Gallery Row" is located on Broad Street. Its galleries grandly display a variety of media from oils to watercolors and blown glass to sculptures, lithographs and prints. Antique collectors also revel in the shops that house museum quality pieces.

Third Street Shopping *(above)*

Twinkling, festive lights adorn trees, storefronts, and plazas during Naples' Festival of Lights and Celebration of Lights. The holiday season officially is launched each November with the tree lighting ceremony by the Mayor. Music and bells are heard from courtyards and plazas, and Santa arrives with snow!

Food and Fun *(opposite, top)*

A hub for upscale shopping and playing, Mercato offers a variety of casual and fine dining options. Stop at The Wine Loft for a glass of imported wine or at Masa for light bites, al fresco. Or, visit Silverspot for a pre-show dinner or cocktails then view a movie in French leather seating.

The Strada at Mercado *(opposite, bottom)*

For the most discriminating who crave luxury shopping, dining, and an entertainment destination steps away from their front door, the residences at Mercato are a natural choice. Ideal for permanent or seasonal dwelling, they feature a rooftop pool and outdoor entertaining amenities.

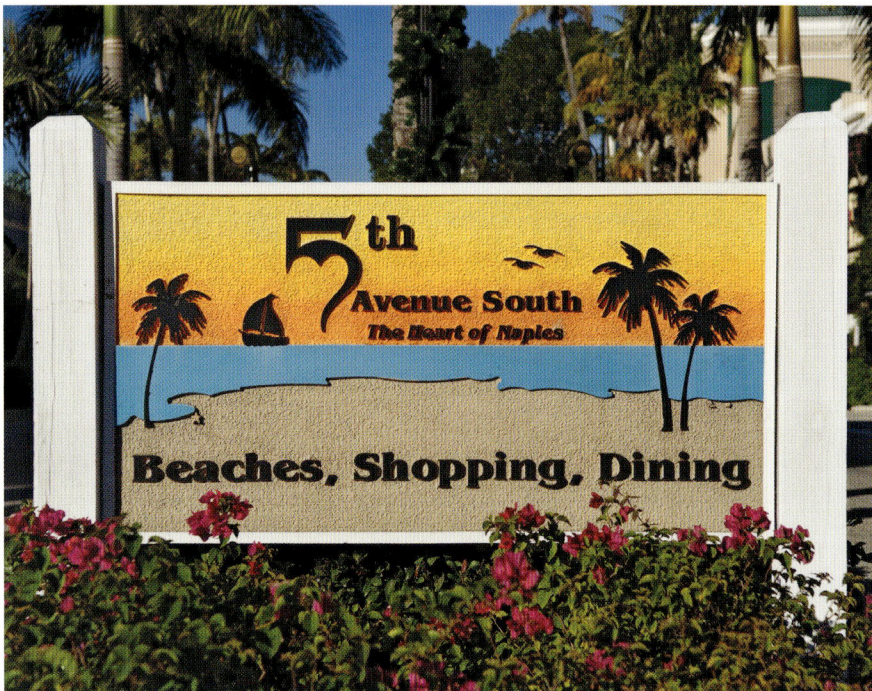

The Heart of Naples (*above and left*)

5th Avenue is the energized core of the City of Naples. Visitors take to the palm tree lined sidewalks during the winter season to take advantage of exclusive lodging, shopping, incomparable indoor and outdoor restaurants, and shows at the Sugden Community Theatre.

Art of 5th

Naples' pulsating art scene extends its passion to the very streets of 5th Avenue, one of three major locales of a thriving art community, ready to feed an art-lover's hunger. Whether you crave fine art, originals, giclees, or limited edition lithographs from masters like Matisse, Picasso or Dali, Naples delivers.

Forbes Star Rated Lodging *(above)*

Rated by Forbes Travel Guide Star Rating as one of 46 Recommended Hotels worldwide, the sophisticated yet unpretentious Inn on Fifth is a premiere 5th Avenue lodging destination offering privacy and superlative accommodations. Amenities include a rooftop pool and luxurious spa.

Essence of 5th *(opposite)*

Oh, if the street could talk. Historians record that in 1932, Charles "Lucky" Lindbergh's plane landed on Naples' downtown thoroughfares – most likely 5th Avenue. Since the 1920s, 5th Avenue has grown from a fledgling town center to one of the most chic, cultural destinations in Southwest Florida.

Dining Options Abound

(top and opposite)

Poinciana, banyan, and palm trees line many of the sidewalks and walkways of bench-lined 5th Avenue. People watching on this picturesque street gives way to cocktails and fine dining at its more than 30 restaurants.

Segway Around Town

Not as difficult as you think, riding a Segway is a unique way to sightsee. After a 30-minute tutorial, you will join Segway Tours of Naples' 90 minute trip to the city's top points of interest. Whir by the iconic Naples Pier, Third Street South, Fifth Avenue South, Cambier Park, Tin City, and the City Dock.

Cigar Bar at Mercato *(top)*

For everything cigar, it's Rocky Patel. Choose from a menu of specialty cocktails like the blueberry-pomegranate martini, reserve wines, cordials, aged whiskey, and the largest selection of fine cigars. Relaxation is mandatory as you settle into richly upholstered leather seats.

Naples Winery *(bottom)*

If you think about local wines from Naples, then tropical wines makes sense, and the proof lies on the tongue. At Naples Winery, find citrus wines made from 100 percent pure, hand-selected Florida citrus fruits, without artificial flavorings. Special processes are used to ferment, age and bottle the wines.

Regina's Ice Cream on 5th Avenue

An old-school ice cream parlor evocative of a fifties spot for icy treats, satisfying Naples' palettes since 1988. Step back in time and find old-fashioned sundaes, ice-cream sodas, malts, and egg crèmes. Grab your best guy or gal, and reminisce with tunes wafting from the juke box.

A Cultural Icon (top)

Artis-Naples is home to the Naples Philharmonic and The Baker Museum. The host of more than 300 concerts, performances, exhibitions, and educational events for children and adults each year, its mission is to create and present world-class visual and performing arts.

Art for the Community (opposite)

With a mission to inspire creativity and awaken curiosity, the three-story, 30,000-square-foot Baker Museum at Artis-Naples strives to be a visual arts resource for people of all ages and backgrounds with a special emphasis on the contributions of modern and contemporary artists.

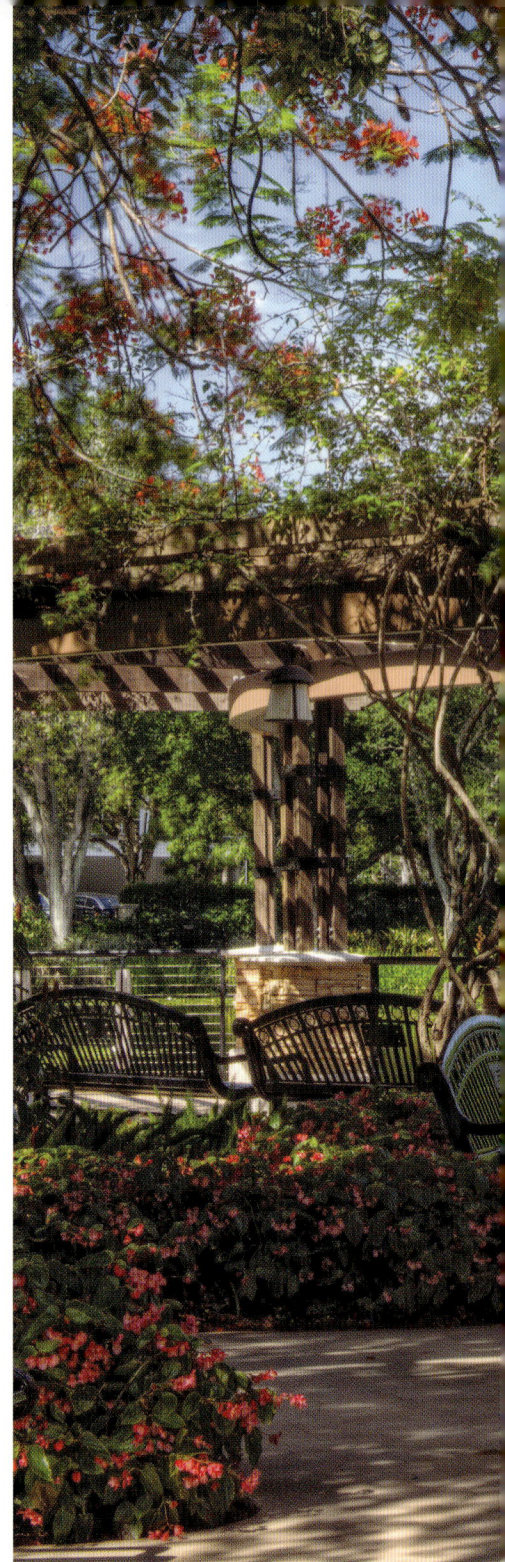

Serenity

The Garden of Hope and Courage at the downtown campus of NCH Healthcare System is set on 2.5 acres and includes an open-air pavilion and healing garden. Designed by Kathy Spalding, it is as a memorial to the courage and grace displayed by Jan Emfield who succumbed to breast cancer in 1994.

A Place of Peace and Refuge

A firm believer in the healing powers of a serene garden setting in which the ill, families, and healthcare providers could meditate and reflect, Emfield's legacy lives on. The sanctuary of the formal garden with the showpiece of a tranquil lake surrounded by trees, provides respite from stress and illness.

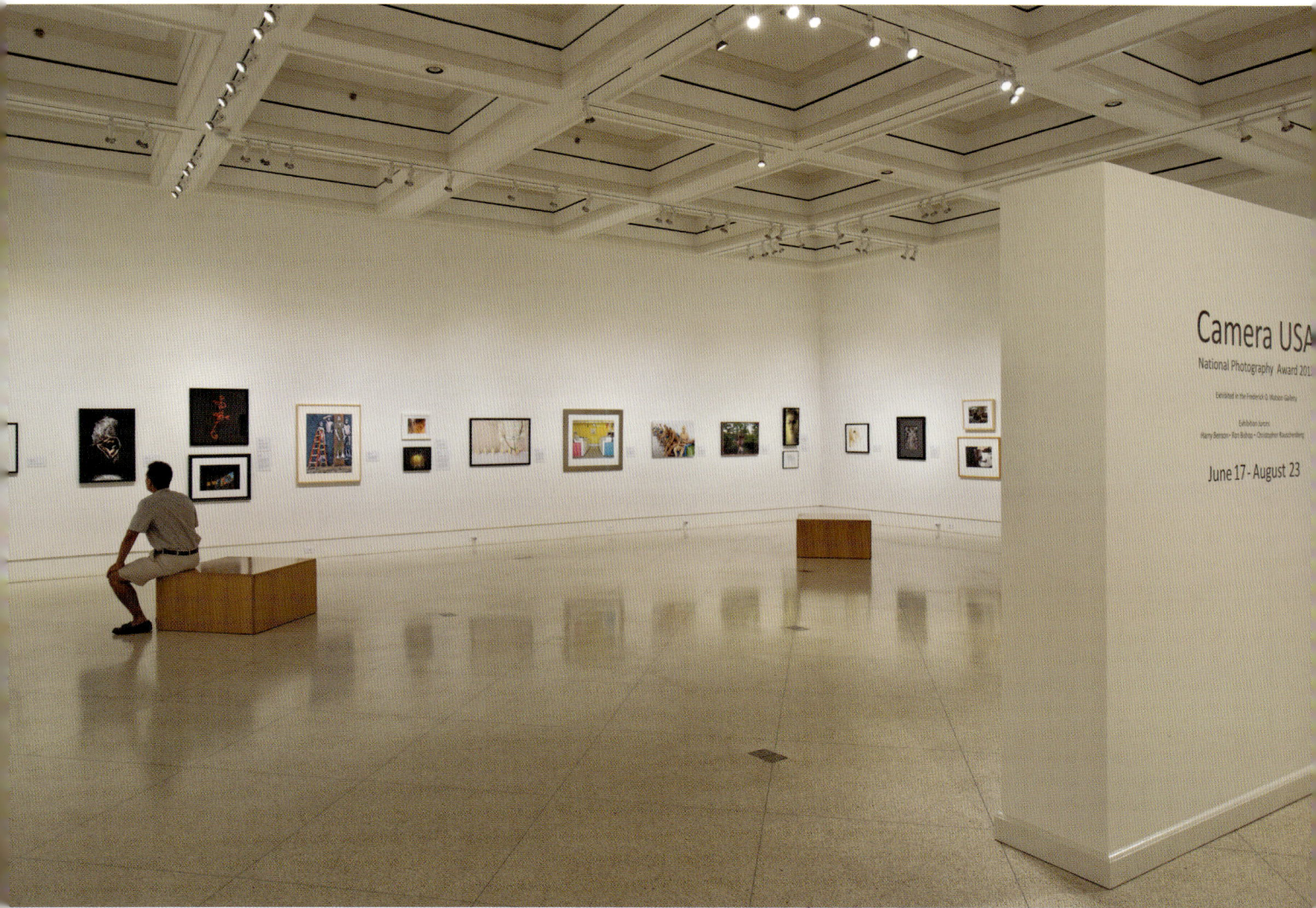

Art and Education *(above and left)*

A gem in Naples' cultural crown, the von Liebig Center was opened in 1998 with a lobby gallery, six studios, a main exhibition gallery, library resource center, and two collection storage vaults. Contemporary American art with a focus on Florida art is offered as well as adult and youth education programs with non-credit, enriching art courses, lectures, and workshops.

South Regional Library *(above and right)*

Opened in May 2009, South Regional Library is the newest of the 10 libraries in Collier County at 30,000 square feet. In addition to 64,000 items, the library has private study rooms, a children's library, a space for teens, and a 300 capacity meeting room. The library hosts well over 140 adult and 70 children and teen programs yearly.

Historic Train Station (*above and left*)

Located at 5th Avenue South and Tenth Street South, the Naples Depot Museum is in the National Register of Historic Places. Once used as the Seaboard Air Line Railway passenger station, the restored depot now houses information about how railroads were used in the late 1800s to facilitate the area's settlement and has memorabilia like the 1955 Bel Air hardtop.

Train Exhibit

Also at the depot is Naples Train Museum, featuring an interactive model layout with nine independent multi-level loops. Children love the selection of interactive buttons from which they, their parents, and grandparents can direct the action of Lionel accessories. It is a bit of nostalgia for model train hobbyists who collected and displayed Lionel brand locomotives and cars.

Educational, Fun, and Inspiring (above)

Located in North Collier Regional Park, the expansive 30,000 square foot C'MON, Golisano Children's Museum of Naples is known as the place where children and families play, learn, and dream together. The two-story building houses 10 permanent and temporary exhibit galleries.

C'MON and Climb (opposite)

One of the more unique play features of the Children's Museum is a banyan tree upon which children can climb and explore. Inside the twists and turns of the 45-foot-tall wonder, youngsters can discover the many animals hiding among its branches and visit the Adopt-A-Pet vet clinic in the tree.

3rd Street Farmers Market
(opposite, top and bottom)

If you are an early riser, there is no better place to go for your morning "cup of Joe" and a gourmet pastry than the Third Street Farmers Market. Open at 7:30 until 11:30 a.m., locals and visitors flock to the site for select, just picked produce.

Art, Art, Everywhere *(above)*

Every first Saturday from November to April, Park Street hosts the best of the Naples Art Association member's offerings at Art in the Park, Naples' oldest art fair, since 1957. Artists display major works of sculpture, hand-crafted jewelry, oils, photography, and more.

Signature Wading Bird (*opposite*)

Awkward looking at best, with their long legs and pink-tinged feet, the wood stork, once considered an endangered species, is now classified as a threatened species. Preferring the habitat of shallow wetlands, they feed by stirring up the sand with their feet. Their wing-span can reach up to six feet.

Fall Pumpkins (*above*)

As the weather descends to comfortable fall temperatures of mid to low 80's, pumpkin patches offer their orbs ready for carving. Dating back to the 17th century, the fun begins after the perfect orange squash has been selected and is ready to be made into a jack-o-lantern.

Naples Depot's Antique Auto Show
(top and bottom)

For the past quarter of a decade, the Naples-Marco Island Region of the Automobile Club of America has played host to one of the nation's most stirring collection of vehicles representative of a bygone era at the Naples Depot's Antique Auto Show.

Wearin' o' the Green (above and right)

The celebration of Irish culture, music, and heritage is serious business in Naples. The St. Patrick's Day Parade is one of the major winter cultural events, drawing crowds of up to 40,000 on-lookers to 5th Avenue to watch floats, marching bands, dancers, and entertainers parade down the avenue.

Covenant Church of Naples PCA

Occupying an entire block, the vibrant congregation serves an average of 450 persons during the summer and 1000 in season. The caring assembly of believers reach out to the community with events like "Project Serve" and the Fall Festival with activities and food for 1200 to 1500 people.

A Church for All

Dedicated February 3, 2008, the 18,870 square foot Moorings Presbyterian Church serves 1,258 members with a seating capacity of 680. The majestic exterior cross points heavenward at 62 feet. Expertly crafted stained glass windows depicting biblical images lend to a reverent ambiance.

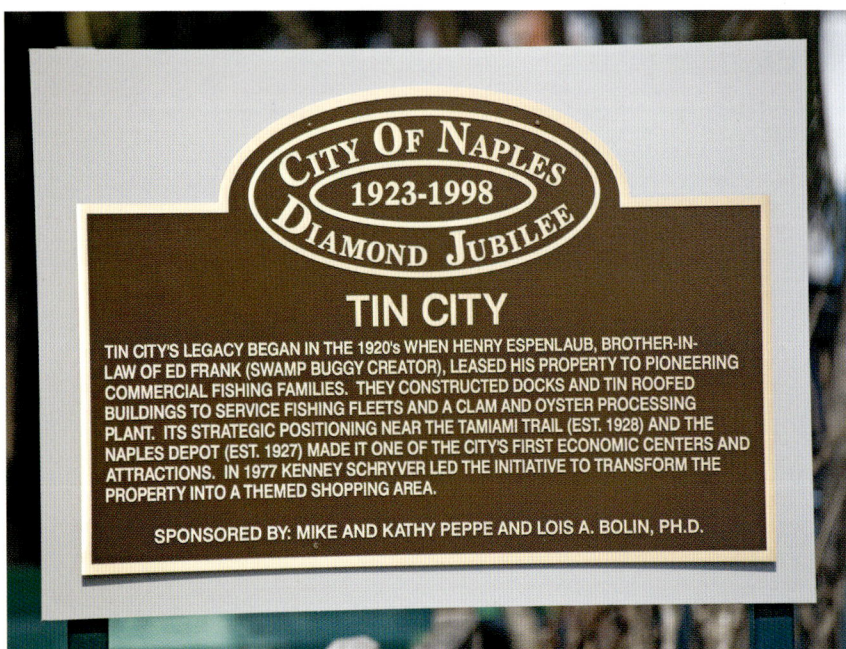

City of Naples
1923-1998
Diamond Jubilee

TIN CITY

TIN CITY'S LEGACY BEGAN IN THE 1920's WHEN HENRY ESPENLAUB, BROTHER-IN-LAW OF ED FRANK (SWAMP BUGGY CREATOR), LEASED HIS PROPERTY TO PIONEERING COMMERCIAL FISHING FAMILIES. THEY CONSTRUCTED DOCKS AND TIN ROOFED BUILDINGS TO SERVICE FISHING FLEETS AND A CLAM AND OYSTER PROCESSING PLANT. ITS STRATEGIC POSITIONING NEAR THE TAMIAMI TRAIL (EST. 1928) AND THE NAPLES DEPOT (EST. 1927) MADE IT ONE OF THE CITY'S FIRST ECONOMIC CENTERS AND ATTRACTIONS. IN 1977 KENNEY SCHRYVER LED THE INITIATIVE TO TRANSFORM THE PROPERTY INTO A THEMED SHOPPING AREA.

SPONSORED BY: MIKE AND KATHY PEPPE AND LOIS A. BOLIN, PH.D.

Tin City *(above and left)*

Originally a 1920's clam shelling and oyster processing plant, the-one-of-a-kind destination exudes charm. Known for providing visitors a glimpse of Naples' maritime past, Tin City is also the home port for sightseeing cruises, dolphin watching, and deep sea fishing charters.

Water Views and Shopping
(opposite, top and bottom)

Eateries line the perimeter of Tin City where succulent seafood or sizzling steaks can be enjoyed while catching the sunset. Home to more than 30 eclectic shops, quaint boardwalks, and a history show-room, this old marine marketplace is a colorful shopping and eating experience.

And the Winner Is… *(above and left)*

Beginning at dusk, the Christmas Boat Parade starts its trek at the upper point of Naples Bay, south of Tin City with judges positioned at Naples City Dock ready to proclaim the best light festooned vessel. Traversing down the bay and past Bay View Park, the lighted boats make their gradual return to the delight of awe-struck crowds.

Boating Amenities *(above and right)*

Olde Naples waterfront features the Naples Boat Club that delivers personalized service while attending to the needs of discriminating boaters. The state-of-the-art marina has a clubhouse, a restaurant, 167 dry rack boat storage boathouses, and a 47 wet slip marina to accommodate boats up to 40 feet long.

Luxe Living

Relaxing from the privacy of exclusive homes, villas, and condominiums like Colony Gardens and Pelican Point West that dot Venetian Bay's edge, lucky residents, many of them seasonal, are able to view a spectacular show of playful dolphins frolicking in tandem in the calm, tepid bay waters.

Venetian Bay

Part of a land purchase that stretched a mile and a quarter along the western shoreline of the Gulf of Mexico, the development of Venetian Bay was the first step in what would be the first Collier County planned unit development district. It now includes bay and gulf front home sites with docks.

The Village Shopping

Step into a world of enchantment at The Village on Venetian Bay, reminiscent of the architecture, mystique, and romance of Venice, Italy. With over 50 boutiques and shops, upscale dining and mesmerizing water views, it is a Naples original.

Shopping and More *(bottom)*

Making world-class shopping a matchless experience, The Village on Venetian Bay offers a schedule of entertaining events year-round. Shoppers revel in Dancing by the Fountain on the north side, and music on the south side, to special holiday events with balloon artists, face painters, and bands.

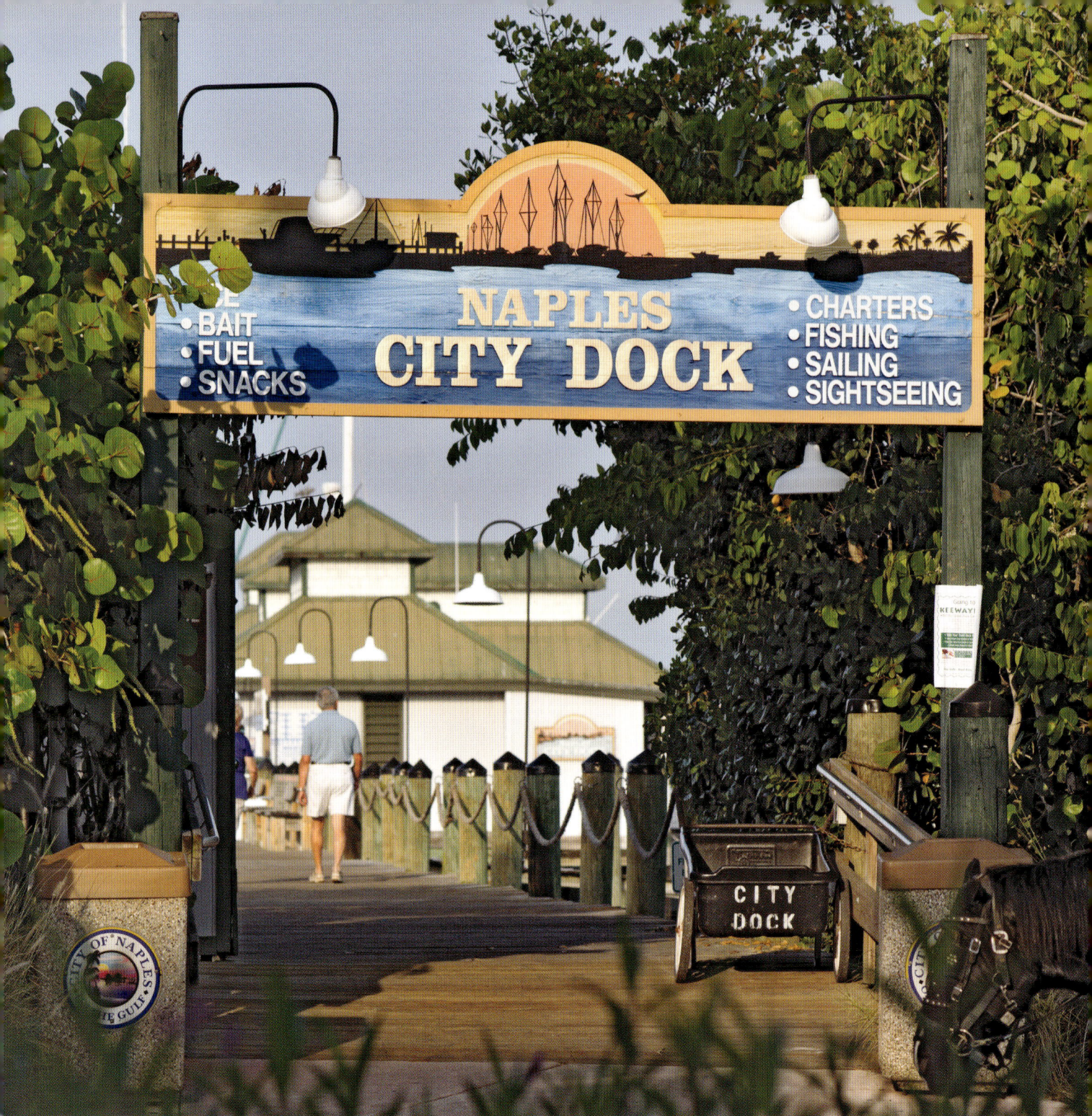

Naples City Dock

Enter the Naples City Dock and find an array of services to keep you occupied all day. Whether you board a sight-seeing boat, sailing vessel, or fishing charter, the dock has you covered. For landlubbers, shopping awaits or dining at the open-air Dock Restaurant that features fresh fish specialties.

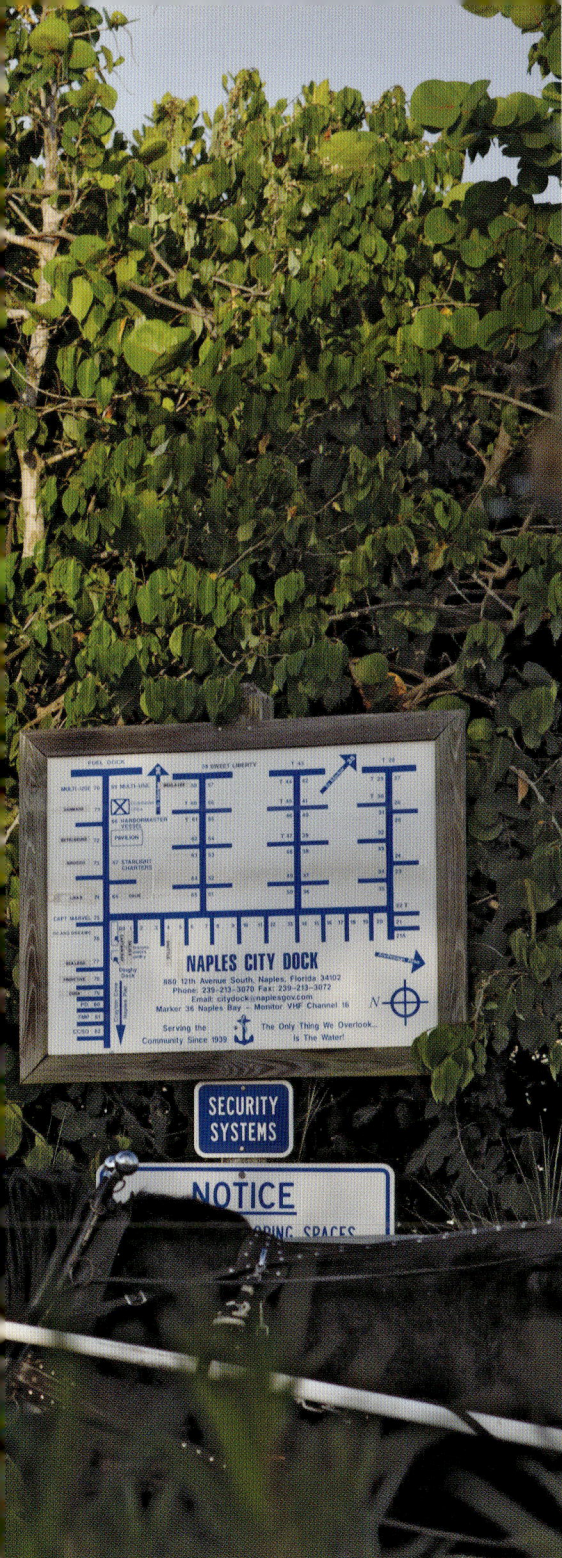

Horse Drawn Carriage *(top)*

Touring Olde Naples in a horse drawn carriage is an enchanting way to see the city. Tours include "the best sunset in the word" as well as the Naples Pier, art galleries, and landmarks. Carriages can also be booked for weddings, birthdays, and other special events.

Clearing Stations *(bottom)*

The City Dock's charter fishing fleet is recognized as one of the very best in the area. The water depth is up to 17-feet at the dock and the channel is about seven feet. After a magnificent day of fishing, convenient cleaning stations are available for filleting your day's catch.

Boating *(top and bottom)*

Whether you are looking for a day of motoring past the million-dollar homes on the Naples Bay waterway, or would rather fish out in the Gulf, there is a boat just right for you. Naples City Dock offers slips for vessels up to 110 feet as well as mooring balls.

Fishing *(opposite)*

It's a balmy day on the Gulf and conditions are perfect for trying out a new net with old tried and true casting techniques to capture baitfish, a prime pre-fishing surfside activity. Whether you throw your net from the Gulf waters shoreline or find your own secret spot, an abundant catch awaits.

Education Through Sailing

The Naples Community Sailing Center is a non-profit organization founded in 1991. Its stated mission is to organize, promote, and develop safe recreational and competitive sailing for area youth and adults on Naples Bay. Boating education instills values, responsibility, and sportsmanship.

Water Activities are a Must

From yacht owners casting off from serene Gulf waters to exciting locales to those who take to the waterways in a single engine motor boat, donning sea-legs is a must-do Naples activity. Nature and sightseeing excursions are also available for die-hard landlubbers.

Fishing From the Pier

From sunrise to sunset, locals and visitors are fond of fishing from Naples' iconic pier. Fishing does not require a state fishing license but hooks are limited to a 5/0 hook size with the hope of limiting the number of pelicans in danger of swallowing the curved metal.

Dolphins *(top and bottom)*

Dolphin sightseeing expeditions let the whole family get up close and personal with the Florida bottle-nose dolphin. Weighing up to 1400 pounds, they are found in waters like the Gulf and at Rookery Bay National Estuarine Research Reserve.

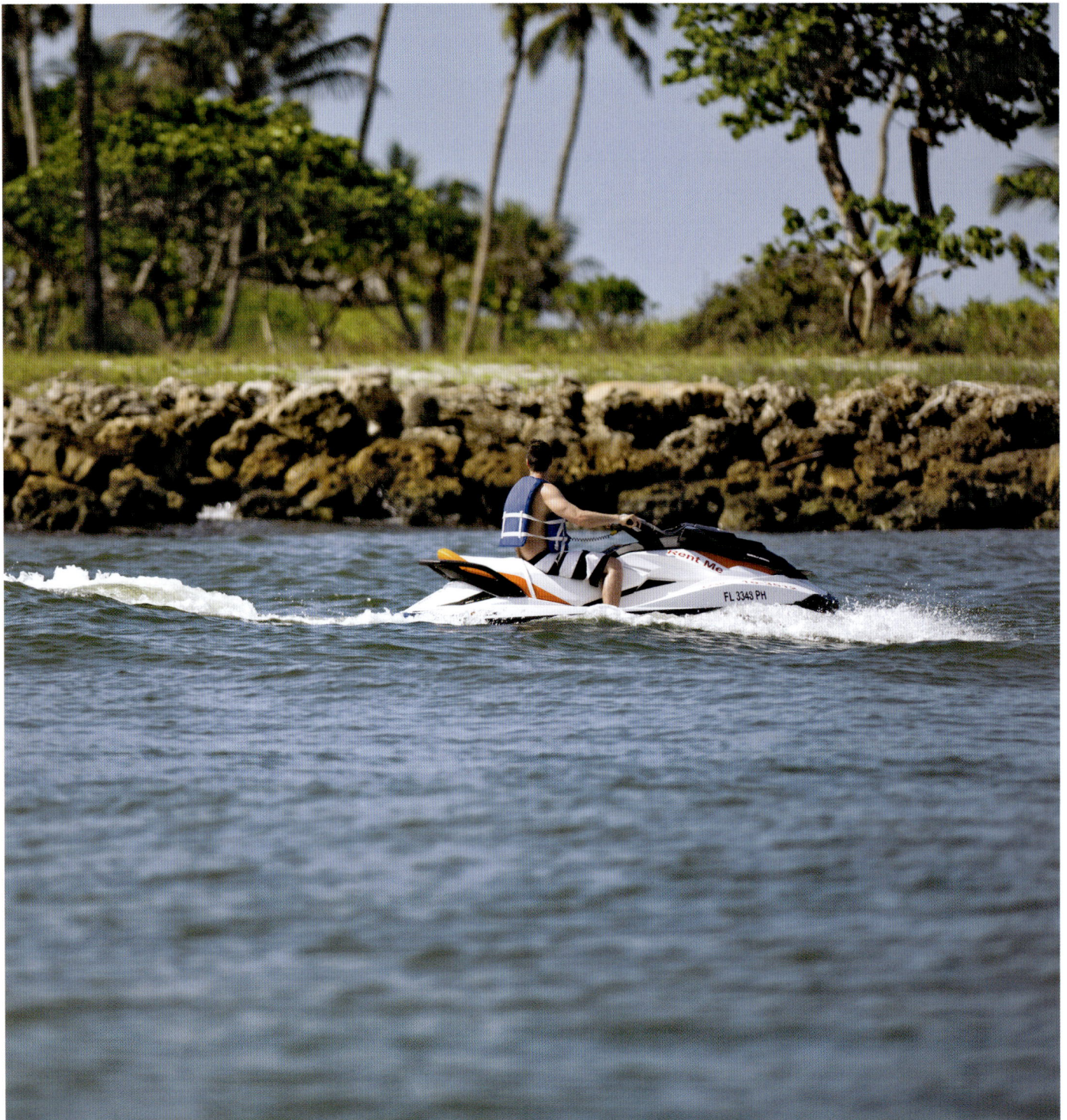

See Nature by Water

A popular water sport, jet skis or wave runners provide a unique encounter with an opportunity to see water nature. Glide through the waters of the Gordon River through Naples Bay south to Keewaydin Island, on tours that depart from the Tin City Marina with experienced guides.

Fly Like a Bird

Jet packs powered by water propel the thrill-seeker through water or up to 30 feet into the air for an unparalleled ride. Easy to learn, experts are on hand to assist for a perfect adventure with the rider who controls turning and elevation. Start in chest high water then graduate to free flight and tricks.

Exclusive Waterfront Living

During the early 1900s John Glen Sample, noted as an early innovator of radio advertising, developed two square miles of marshland and turned it into six hundred single family building lots in the section known as Port Royal. Most every estate has waterfront with deep water access.

Destination for the Elite (above)

Perfectly manicured gardens, majestic banyan trees, and tasteful landscaping adorn homes in the prestigious Port Royal neighborhood in downtown Naples. Owned by company executives, celebrities and sports figures, the area is considered the most exclusive in Naples. Port Royal is bordered on the west by the Gulf of Mexico with canals and the Naples Bay bordering other home sites.

Community Club (right)

Signs announcing Port Royal streets with pirate-inspired names and art recall a time gone by when ships were moored on the shoreline after arduous sea excursions. Residents are privy to membership at the Port Royal Club, established in 1959. From twilight cocktails to sumptuous beachside dinners, the highest quality service and attention to detail is the standard.

LANTERN LANE

Celebrating Freedom

Opened in October 2009, the 50-acre Freedom Park is located near the corner of Goodlette-Frank Road and Golden Gate Parkway. The park features a five-acre lake, a 3500-foot-long boardwalk that was constructed over a natural wetland, bike and walking trails, a visitor's center, and much more.

Our Natural Resources *(top and bottom)*

The land upon which Freedom Park sits was purchased by Collier County in 2004 for a reported cost of $19.2 million. It took 17 months to erect the park that cost $12.3 million, funded in part by the Collier County's Conservation Collier Program.

Homage to Non-native Wildlife

(above and opposite, top)

Two bronze sculptures greet passers-by on Mooring Line Drive. One is a friendly hippopotamus and the other, a procession of African elephants headed by a trumpeting leader. The elephants, once known as the "Chardonnay Pachyderms," are a Naples landmark.

Naples' Flora (right)

Trees like the blue jacaranda or fern tree is a sub-tropical species that sports a bounty of vivid blue flowers that are long-lasting, even in hot climates. Native to South America, the tree prefers no-frost zones and can be found in full bloom adorning Naples' lush city and private landscapes.

Gardens with Latitude *(above and left)*

Naples Botanical Garden, on a 170-acre site south of Old Naples, boasts seven habitats including six cultivated gardens, 2.5 miles of walking trails, and 90-acres of restored native preserve. A place of exploration and refuge from the busyness of life for adults as well as children, it offers educational lectures, a summer camp, and is available for social functions.

Up Close *(opposite, top and bottom)*

Stroll through Pfeffer-Beach Butterfly Garden to see an array of beautiful Florida butterflies. Or cross the boardwalk over the Water Garden and enjoy tropical water lilies, both delicate in appearance and hardy in their ability to subsist in their environment.

Protected Haven (above and left)

Rookery Bay Estuarine Research Reserve, one of the few mangrove estuaries on the continent, is located at the northern end of the Gulf Coast's Ten Thousand Islands. The 110,000-acre sanctuary for 150 bird species, endangered animals, and native wildlife also houses an Environmental Learning Center that is a hub for research, interactive exhibits, an aquarium, and 140-seat auditorium.

Protecting the Environment
(opposite, top and bottom)

The Conservancy of Southwest Florida works to preserve and protect the land, waters, and native species of plants and animals found in five Southwest Florida counties. Patrons enjoy relaxing electric boat cruises up the Gordon River with the captain as tour guide identifying the variety of native plants and wildlife like shorebirds, birds of prey, and manatee.

Naples Zoo *(top)*

Along with viewing Naples Zoo's herd of seven giraffe, guests can experience the thrill of hand-feeding the stately creatures. From 10 a.m. to 3 p.m. daily, zoo visitors have the opportunity to get up close to the world's tallest animals as these giants lean down to slurp a snack using their 18" long tongues.

Naples Zoo Theater *(bottom)*

Safari Canyon's open-air theater allows guests to view animals not displayed in other parts of the zoo. Using both live camera action and supplemental video footage, the wondrous world of wildlife is presented in fun ways. Hawks soaring overhead to reptiles crawling on stage assist guests in understanding nature.

Zoo Tour Boats

Throughout the day, the Primate Expedition Cruise departs the dock to glide through and explore the zoo's islands inhabited by monkeys, lemurs, and apes. While skimming past the islands, guests enjoy learning fascinating facts about the world of primates including their amazing natural abilities.

A Time to Feed

Snowy white egrets alight onto the banks of tranquil inland waters and canals and extend their sinewy necks in readiness of spotting prey during morning or early evening feedings. In spectacular flight, a wide-mouthed tarpon becomes airborne to attack unwitting bait fish.

King of Florida's Predators *(top)*

An American alligator holds court as the quintessential marauder in its habitat of swamps, marshes, lakes, ponds, rivers, and coastal brackish waters. A vital contributor to the ecology of the wetlands, keeping the prey population in check, the slow-moving reptiles live an average of 35 to 50 years.

The Littlest Predator *(bottom)*

After incubating for 60 days, baby alligators hatch from their eggs and stay in their mothers' vicinity for years. They prefer natural land habitats with temperatures of 75 to 105 degrees Fahrenheit and water habitats of 75 to 80 degrees Fahrenheit.

Bird of Prey (top)

Ospreys are year-round Florida nesting residents with some migrating to rivers, lakes, ponds, and the Gulf coast that provide food for themselves and their young. Their nests are found in the dead tops of living trees, in strong dead trees, or atop high poles.

Florida Turtles (bottom)

The red-bellied turtle is identifiable by the orange and red coloration on the underside of their shell, called the plastron or belly and also by the pattern of the yellow lines on its head. Brightly colored as juveniles, adult males average seven to nine inches and females are usually 11 to 13 inches.

Wildlife (opposite)

Known as a large bird of prey, some ospreys are as large as two feet long with imposing wingspans of six feet with a distinctive black line that extends behind the eye. The underside of each of the toes is covered with short spines that are necessary to grasp wet fish.

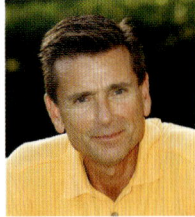

Randall Perry

Trained at both the Art Institute of Fort Lauderdale and Randolph Technical Institute, Randall is widely known as a leader in his field offering quality, award winning photography for over 27 years.

A specialist in architectural photography, Randall's work has appeared internationally, nationally, and regionally in books on design related subjects and in countless consumer and trade publications.

He has photographed the United States Culinary Team, in Birmingham and London, England and has captured the grandeur of locales like the resorts of Sequoia and Yosemite National Park as well as private homes, hotels, and commercial projects all along the east coast.

Originally from upstate New York, in 1995, Randall opened an office on Cape Cod, Massachusetts to better serve his growing client base in that region. In 1999, he discovered the matchless, natural beauty of Southwest Florida and opened a third office in Bonita Springs. Visit www.randallperry.com to learn more.

Jean Amodea

Originally from Hackensack, New Jersey, Jean earned a B.A. in English from William Patterson University and an M.A. in Administration & Supervision from Kean University. As a teacher, then principal in schools for handicapped students, Jean's experiences afforded a glimpse into the sensitivities and psychology of the human spirit. After relocating to Naples in 1997, she opened a satellite office of New York entertainment giant, Peter Duchin. Jean performs with her husband Ron, a career musician, and their various bands for corporate and private clients. With a penchant for writing, Jean is an independent writer for the *Naples Daily News* and its community publications, for *NCH Newsletter* and the Jewish Federation *Star*. Currently, she creates print and video memoirs for private clients. Ever-caring for the well-being of children, Jean is a volunteer Guardian ad Litem, serving as the voice of vulnerable children to Collier County courts. Visit www.naplesbuzz.info to learn more about Jean.